Signs Resource Book

Signs Resource Book
Copyright © 2022 all rights reserved

Purpose of this book

The purpose of this resource book is to learn signs ranging from street signs, store signs, and COVID 19 signs. Signs give us directions and instructions that tell us to do something. Learning these signs is a life skill that can help students practice their English skills. Each page will show a sign with its meaning. Some pages will show examples of an instruction. All photos were taken by Dara K. Fulton from different cameras and various environments. This book is a good resource for ESL students of all English levels who are unfamiliar with certain signs. This is also good for students who want to improve their literacy skills in identifying different signs and reading instructions.

1. Street Signs

Stop sign

All traffic must stop

Stop All Way

All traffic must stop in all directions

Stop No Left Turn

Traffic must stop and can't make a left turn

Stop No Right Turn

Traffic must stop and can't make a right turn

Stop Ahead

A stop sign is ahead, traffic must prepare to stop

Two way traffic

Traffic that goes in two different directions

Two way traffic ahead

Traffic will go in two different directions

Signal Ahead

Traffic must prepare to see this signal:

Red means to stop

Yellow means to yield (wait)

Green means to go

Walk signal

To walk across the street

Do not walk signal

Do not cross the street

Crosswalk button

Press the button for walk signal

Example of a crosswalk

Push the button and wait for WALK signal

Sidewalk

A path on the side of a street for pedestrians to walk

Example of standing on a sidewalk

Sidewalk Closed

A sidewalk is closed and pedestrians must follow the instructions on the sign

Sidewalk Closed Use Other Side

Use the sidewalk opposite of the closed sidewalk

Sidewalk Closed Use Temporary Sidewalk

Use sidewalk that is open for a limited period of time

Sidewalk Closed

Cross the street at the crosswalk and use <u>other side</u>

(sidewalk that is opposite of the closed sidewalk)

Cross the street at the crosswalk and use other side

Which WAY?

One Way

To go in one direction

Examples of One Way signs

One way RIGHT

One way LEFT

Straight Ahead Only
To go straight ahead, no turns

Right Turn Only
Can only make right turns

Intersection Lane Control

To show the direction of each lane

1. Left turns only

2. Left turn or continue straight ahead

3. Straight ahead only

4. Right turns only

All Traffic Right

All traffic must go right

Two Direction Arrow

Must allow another car to enter an intersection or stop before turning right or left

Divided Highway

Traffic moving in the opposite direction is divided by a barrier (or median)- Keep right to the center of the road

Pedestrian Crossing

People can walk on the side of a street

No Pedestrian Crossing

People can't walk on the side of a street

No Pedestrian Crossing

People must walk on the crosswalk to the left

No U Turn

Can't make a U turn on a street

No Right Turn

Can't turn right

Left Lane Must Turn Left

Must turn left on the left lane

No Turns

No turns in all directions

No Trucks

No trucks can drive on a street except for local deliveries

Truck Route

Trucks can stop or make deliveries on local streets

No Thru Truck Traffic

No trucks can drive through a place (example: a town)

Local Traffic Only

Traffic for people who live in a particular area or is doing business in the area

Passenger Cars Only

Cars with passengers can drive on the street (no trucks)

Keep Intersection Clear

Must stop before an intersection, a stop line or crosswalk

Do Not Enter

No traffic or pedestrians can enter on a street or sidewalk

Speed Bump

A bump on a street to prevent speeding on streets

Must slow down at 20 miles per hour (M.P.H)

A bump on a street

Example of a BUMP sign on a street

Your Speed

Shows the amount of speed you are driving on a street in Miles Per Hour (M.P.H)

Red left arrow: Can't make a left turn

Green left arrow: Can make a left turn

Left Turn Signal

Turn left at signal

Stop Here On Red

Stop on right lane when there is a red signal

Stop Here on Red Signal

Stop at a red signal

Yield

To slow down and let drivers, pedestrians or cyclists to pass by

Side Road Right

A warning sign of a side road that will enter a highway or an intersection

Side Road Left

A warning sign of a side road that will enter a highway or an intersection

Cross Road Sign

A warning sign that another road ahead will cross the road or highway

Shared Roadway Ahead

A shared street for different types of transportation (cars or bicycles) is ahead

Bicycle lane

A lane on a street to ride a bicycle

Example of a bicycle lane and a crosswalk

Shared lane

A street shared by cars and bicycles

Example of a shared lane with cars and a bicycle

*Some streets will not have a bicycle lane but is still shared

Use Ped (Pedestrian) Signal

Push button for walk signal: this is used to walk or ride a bicycle across the street

People on bicycles must allow pedestrians to walk first before they can ride across the street

Share the Road

A street shared by pedestrians and bicycles

Speed is 5 Miles Per Hour (M.P.H.)

Turning Vehicles Right-Yield to Pedestrians and Bicycles

Traffic must wait for people and bicycles to cross before turning right

Bicycle Wrong Way

Bicycles are not allowed to ride in the direction of the sign that is facing the left or right side of a street

No Bicycles Allowed

Bicycles are not allowed to ride on a particular street

Left turns only

Traffic can only make left turns at an intersection

Left or Straight Lane

Go straight or make a left turn on this lane

School Crossing

A warning sign to let traffic know that it is approaching a place where children are crossing a street

An example of a SCHOOL crossing sign on a street

Playground (Playground Ahead)

A warning sign to let traffic know that it is approaching a place children play

Neighborhood Slow Zone

A specific area of a neighborhood with reduced speed limits to keep people safe

End School Speed Limit

Speed limit ends for streets in a school zone

Don't Block The Box

Vehicles should not block an intersection, crosswalks or bike lanes

Hospital

A hospital or a medical facility is ahead

Wheelchair Traffic

No traffic is allowed in an area that is for wheelchair accessibility

Hidden Driveway

A warning sign for traffic that a residential driveway is ahead

Speed Limit

The amount of traffic speed on a street

City Speed Limit-Photo Enforced

The amount of traffic speed on a street in Miles Per Hour (M.P.H.)

Photo Enforced

A camera will take a photo of a car's license plate if the car is speeding

The driver of the car will get a ticket and must pay a fee

Dead End

A warning sign at the beginning of a street to let traffic know that a street, road or a path will end

End

Same as Dead End, a warning sign at the beginning of a street to let traffic know that a street, road or a path will end

Detour

A warning sign to let traffic know that the direction of a road or a street will change

An alternative route is ahead because of construction

Road Narrows

A warning sign to let traffic know that the road ahead will become narrow (not wide)

Road Work Ahead

Work on a road is ahead

Traffic must follow the directions on construction signs or from a construction worker or flagger

Flagger: a person who directs traffic when there is construction on a street

Lane Closed Ahead

Lane or street is closed

Merge Left

Two roadways will merge (come together) into one road

Drivers must prepare to merge from one road into another

Slow

A warning for drivers to slow down

Work Zone Ahead

Work on a road is ahead

Traffic must share the road with bicycles

No Parking Anytime

Temporary Construction Regulation

No cars can park in an area because it is a construction site

No Standing Anytime

No cars can park, wait or make deliveries in a particular location

No Parking

No cars can park at certain times of the day

Truck Loading Only

No standing for all vehicles except trucks

Trucks can load and unload at the times on the sign

No Standing

No cars can park at a location for a specific reason

Security Checkpoint: a place cars are inspected for security

reasons

No Stopping Anytime: No cars can stop at a specific location

Ambulance Only: only ambulances (emergency vehicles) can

stop (usually at a hospital)

No Standing

No cars can park at a certain location for a specific reason

Fire Zone: an area for the fire department to access buildings

No Engine Idling

Vehicles cannot idle: a vehicle that leaves its engine on when it is not moving

Max Fine $2000: a driver must pay a maximum fee of $2000 dollars if their vehicle is caught idling

No Parking

Cannot leave a car in a specific area at any time of the day

No Parking

Cannot leave a car in an active driveway

24 Hour Active Driveway: a driveway that is working 24 hours in a day

What is a highway?

A high speed roadway that connects cities and towns

What is an expressway?

A high speed highway that has four or more lanes

You may see the following signs on a highway or an expressway

Speed Limit: Limit of speed that is checked by street radar

Added Lane

A new lane is added to the main highway for traffic to enter from the side road

No merge is necessary and drivers can continue to drive onto a new lane

Merge Left-Merge Right

Two roadways will merge (come together) into one road

Drivers must prepare to merge from one road into another

Left Reverse Turn Ahead

A warning that two turns or curves are ahead when making a left turn

Winding Road

A warning that the road ahead will have three or more curves in a row

Exit

To leave a highway, expressway or a road
The arrow shows the direction of the exit

Exit Right

Ramp

A sharp curve ahead to exit or enter a new lane on a highway

Double Arrow

A car can pass another vehicle on either side of the lane

Limited Sight Distance

A warning for drivers that there is limited sight between you and traffic ahead, to drive with caution

Example of limited sight distance

Uneven Lanes

A warning for drivers that there are uneven lanes ahead because of construction

Fallen Rocks

A warning for drivers that rocks may fall onto a road from either side of the road

Shoulder Work

A warning sign that road work is ahead on the shoulder

Shoulder is an emergency lane outside of a main road

Example of a shoulder

Raise Plow

A warning for drivers that snow clearing vehicles are ahead

These vehicles help raise snow plows that often get damaged from construction plates hidden under snow or speed bumps

Example of a construction plate

Example of a snow plow

No Outlet

Used at an entrance to a street or a network of streets that have no other exits

Road Work

A warning for drivers that in one mile there is road work ahead

Do Not Cross Double Solid Line

Drivers cannot cross the double solid line EXCEPT to make a left turn to enter or leave a highway

Example of a double solid line

No Trucks Buses Trailers Left Lane

Certain vehicles cannot drive on the left lane

High Occupancy Vehicle (HOV) Lane

A restricted traffic lane that is reserved for vehicles with a certain amount of passengers

Low clearance

Signs that restrict vehicles to drive on certain roads or under a bridge of certain height or width requirements

Sharp Curve

A sharp left curve is ahead

Left Curve Ahead

A left curve is ahead

Must reduce speed to 25 Miles Per Hour (M.P.H)

Low Bridge Ahead

A bridge that has a certain height

Cars must meet the height restrictions to pass under the bridge

To East To West

Directions on a highway or an expressway

Exit Only

A lane to exit a highway or an expressway

Emergency Parking

An area to park when there is an emergency

Parking Area

An area to park a vehicle

Weigh Station

An area on a highway for vehicles (mostly trucks) to be weighed

Service Road

A road that is off a highway for vehicles that needs service

(example: fixing a flat tire)

Road Service By Permit Only

A service that is certified to help drivers who need service on their vehicle (example: towing service)

Slippery When Wet

A warning for drivers that slippery or wet conditions are ahead

Railroad Crossing

Drivers must stop and wait for signal to cross railroad tracks

Deer Crossing

A warning sign that prepares drivers to stop if a deer crosses a road

Pedestrian Crossing Ahead

A crosswalk or a lane is ahead for people to walk

Unlawful to Litter

It is against the law to litter (throw garbage on a highway)

Fine: a fee a person must pay for breaking the law

Example of litter (garbage)

2. Transportation Signs

Cars

Four wheeled vehicles that are run by engines and can carry two or more people

To JFK Airport- Exit Right

Drivers must exit right to get to John F Kennedy (JFK) airport

Cars are driving on the expressway to
John F. Kennedy Airport

Airplane

A flying vehicle with wings that flies in the air

Airport

A place to take an airplane

Terminal

A building at an airport where passengers can get to their flights

Arriving Flights

The place airplanes land

Departing Flights

The place airplanes leave

Example of an airport terminal

Seats

Something to sit on (example: chair)

Each seat is assigned to passengers

Life vest under seat

A sleeveless jacket that inflates to prevent a person from drowning in water

Fasten seat belt whilst seated

To close a seatbelt while seated

Seat belt: a safety device to prevent a passenger from getting hurt

No Smoking in Lavatory

Cannot smoke cigarettes in the bathroom (lavatory)

Lock door

To fasten a door that prevents someone from opening it

Pull the lever right to lock the door

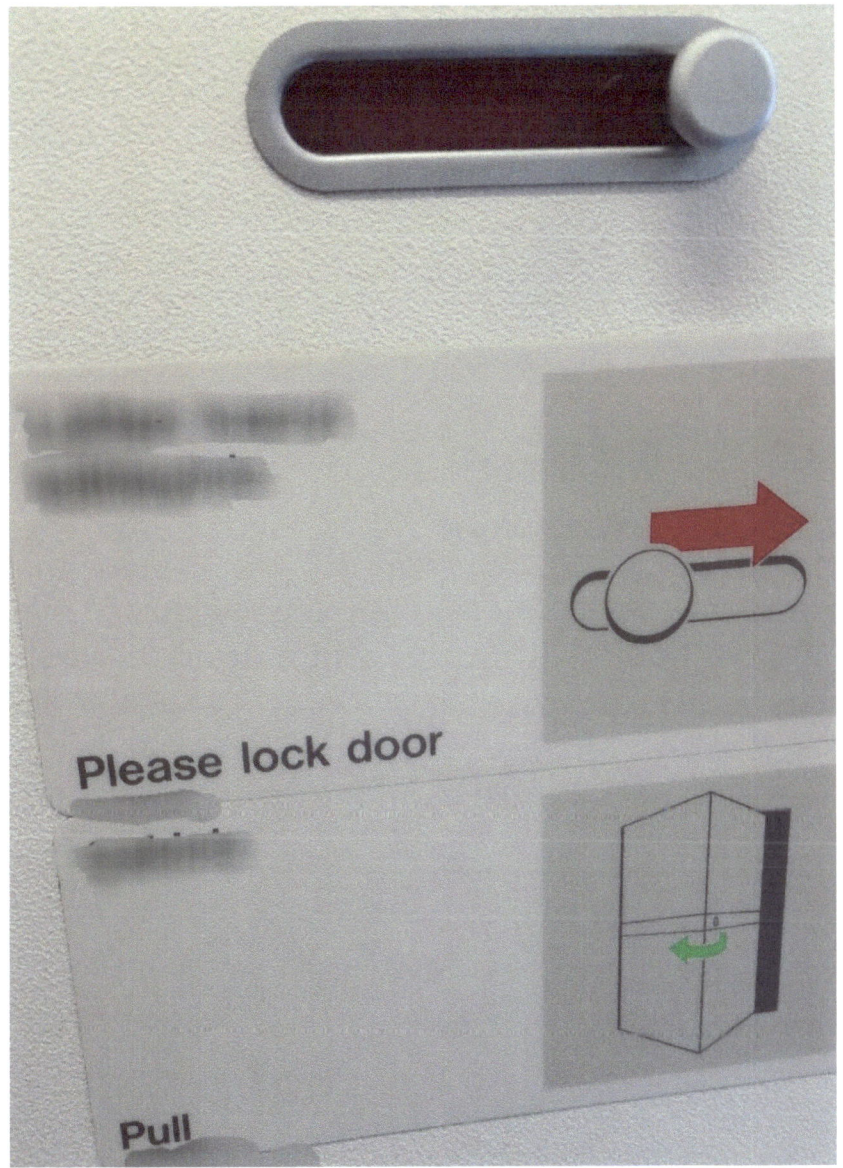

Please lock door

Pull

Pull lever left to open the door

Inside an airplane bathroom

Push button to flush the toilet

Sink: a basin with water and a drain to wash

(left) Hot water

(right) Cold water

Soap: liquid to wash hands

Taxi Line/Taxi Stand

A place street taxis line up to wait for passengers

Taxi

A car service that picks up passengers to take them to their destination

24 Hours Park

Park: To stop a car and leave it on a street or in a parking lot

24 HRS: 24 hours in a day

Parking lot

A place to park a car

Row

A section in a parking lot

Example of rows in a parking lot

Park Open Late

A parking lot that is open late

No Parking Tow Away Zone

No parking allowed in an area where cars are towed

Tow: to pull away a vehicle using a chain

No Parking on Certain Days

No cars can park on Saturday

No cars can park on Monday and Tuesday

Funeral Parking Only

Parking for cars that are for a funeral home only

Fees for any towed cars must be paid by the car owner

Funeral home: a place to prepare the dead for burial or cremation

Flowers are used at a funeral home when a person dies

Share the Road

A street shared by cars and bicycles

Subway

A place to take the train

Subway Train

A train that runs underground and above ground

Train: a series of cars connected together that takes passengers from one place to another

Inside a train car

Underground subway station

A subway station that is under the ground

No Downtown Train at this Station: no trains going downtown will stop at this station

Elevated subway station

A subway station above ground

Bus

A large vehicle that transports passengers from one place to another

Stop Requested

A signal that alerts the bus driver to stop at the next bus stop

Push Button for Bus Arrivals Audio

Push the button and wait for the bus to arrive

Audio (voice) to announce the bus arrival

Buses Only

A lane for buses only

Bus Lanes Photo Enforced

A camera will take a photo of a car's license plate if a car is in a bus lane

The driver will get a ticket and must pay a fee

Buses Only Signal

A signal for buses only

Ferry Ahead

A ferry terminal is ahead

Ferry

A type of boat that takes passengers across a body of water

3. Instructions

Push

To press a door open

Example of pushing a door open using the door handle

Exit

To leave

Not An Exit

Not a place to leave

Please Use Other Door

To use another door to enter

Automatic Door-Keep Moving

Door opens on its own, walk inside when it opens

Automatic Sliding Door

Door slides open on its own when walking towards it

Do Not Enter: Cannot go inside

Automatic Caution Door

Pay attention to door that opens on its own when walking towards it

In Emergency Push to Open

Push the door open when there is an emergency

Main Entrance Around Corner

To enter inside a place around the corner

Wheelchair Accessible

A place that has an entrance for people who uses a wheelchair or have a disability

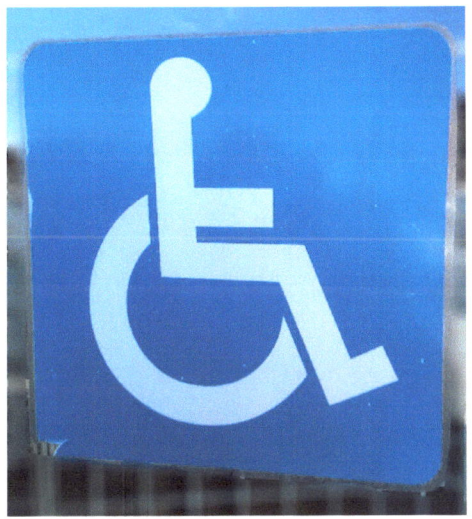

Do Not Chain Bike to the Gate

Cannot chain a bike (bicycle) to the gate or it will be clipped off (removed)

Example of a chained bike

Positively No Ball Playing Allowed

Cannot play ball (basketball, football, or baseball) outside of the building

Residential Block No Horns Please

No horns (noise) on a block with residences (houses and apartments)

Caution Watch Your Step

Pay attention when entering or exiting a place

Please Curb Your Dog

Do not allow your dog to relieve itself on the street

No Dogs Allowed

No Soliciting

A request for businesses or individuals not to sell or bother anyone at a residence or a business

Security Camera

A hidden camera that protects a business or a home from criminal activity

Trash Can

A can or a bin to throw away things we don't want (*waste* is the same as trash)

Examples of trash

Trash or waste are things that we throw away

Garbage are certain things that we throw away (old food, clothes, paper)

No Dumping-Violators Will Be Prosecuted

Anyone who leaves garbage in a place that is not allowed will get in trouble; it's against the law

Example of dumping garbage

Fire Hydrant

A pipe in a street that provides water to put out fires

Example of a fire hydrant

Sprinklers Throughout Building

A device in a building that releases water when there is a fire

Fire Alarm

An alarm to let people know there is a fire

Danger

Do Not Walk On Grill-Slippery When Wet

Do not walk on grill (grate) when it is wet

Slippery: wet surface that makes it difficult to stand or walk on

Post No Bills

Do not put any advertisements on a wall

Danger

Construction Area -Keep Out

Do not enter a construction area because it is dangerous

Example of a construction area

Caution-Hard Hat Required in this Area

Must wear a hard hat to protect your head

Example of construction workers wearing a hard hat

Danger-Eye Protection Required in this Area

Must wear protective eye glasses to protect your eyes

Example of a construction area where eye protection is required

Pedestrian Walkway

An area for people to walk at or near a construction site

Example of a pedestrian walkway

There is snow on the pedestrian walkway

The Public Restroom

A public restroom is a bathroom that is available for the public

Stall

Toilet

A stall is a private area with a toilet

A toilet is used to relieve yourself

Please Do Not Throw Paper Towels in Toilet

Do not throw paper towels (tissues) in the toilet

This can cause the toilet to clog (something that blocks the toilet to flush)

Soap Dispenser

Soap is released when hand is under the dispenser

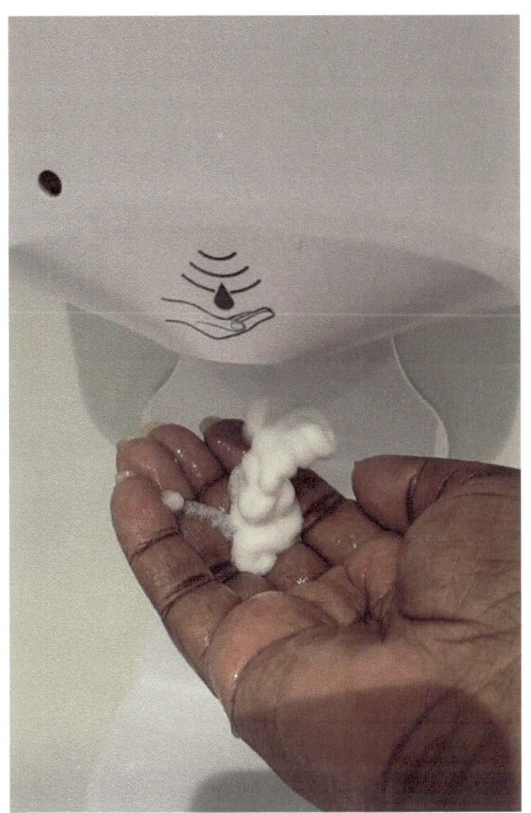

Sink

A basin to wash your hands

Please Wash Your Hands

After using the restroom use soap to wash your hands

Example of washing hands

Hand Dryer

A device to dry your hands

Out of Order

The toilet is not working-cannot use

Restroom

Restroom for men, women, and people with disabilities

Restroom

A restroom for women and women with disabilities only

Baby changing area: an area inside the restroom to change a baby's diaper

This Room is for your Convenience-Please Keep it Clean

Keep the restroom clean for everyone's needs

Beach

A place with sand, a shoreline, and an ocean

Danger-Beach Closed

The beach is closed

No swimming or entering the water is allowed

No Lifeguard on Duty-Swimming or bathing prohibited

No swimming or bathing (an area for the public to bathe/wash) is allowed

Lifeguard: a person trained to rescue people who cannot swim or is drowning

Lifeguard on duty: lifeguard is working

No Jumping or Diving from Pier

Cannot jump or dive into the water from the pier

Pier

A platform with pillars that extends from the shore to the water

Example of a pillar

4. Store Signs-COVID 19 Instructions

Supermarket

A large store that sells food

Aisle

A section in a supermarket that shows the items in that section

List of food items in an aisle

Food examples

Potatoes and onions   Chicken

Milk

Bread

Types of Aisles

An aisle that has a specific type of food

Sushi: a Japanese dish made from raw fish, rice and other ingredients

Example of sushi

Deli: a store or section of a supermarket that sells cold cuts, sandwiches, and salads

Cold cuts: sliced meat that is cold, cooked or processed

Ham	Turkey

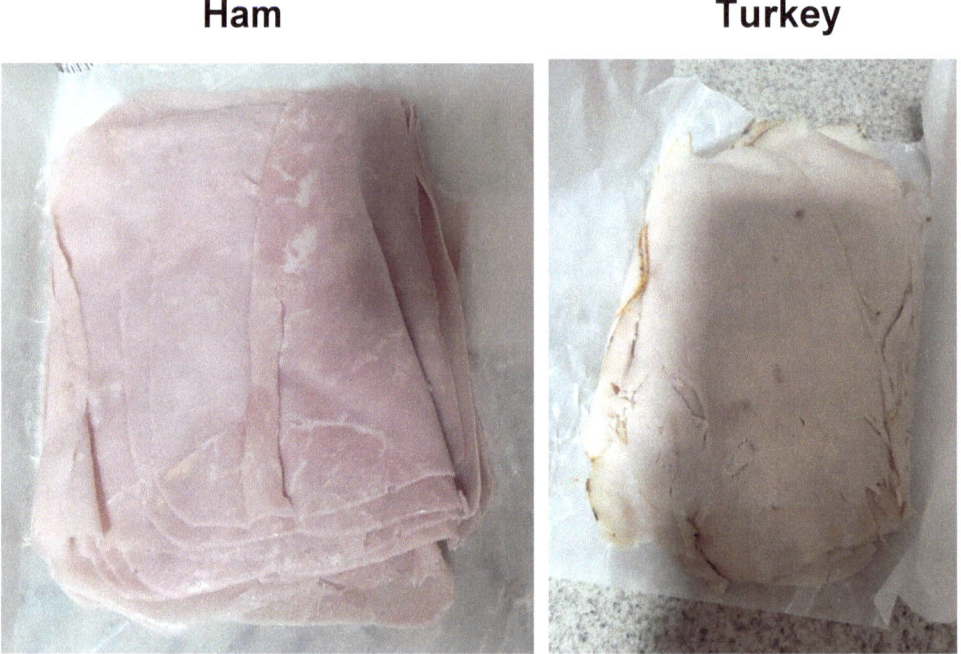

Sandwich: a type of food with cold cut meat, cheese, lettuce and tomato between two slices of bread

Wrap: a type of food with cold cut meat, cheese, lettuce and tomato rolled in a soft tortilla

Example of a turkey wrap

Health Food Store

A store that sells food that is healthy for the body

Examples of health food

Limes, lemons, pineapple

Tea with lemon

Green vegetables

Vitamins

Pills with vitamins (substances) to help the body feel healthy and strong

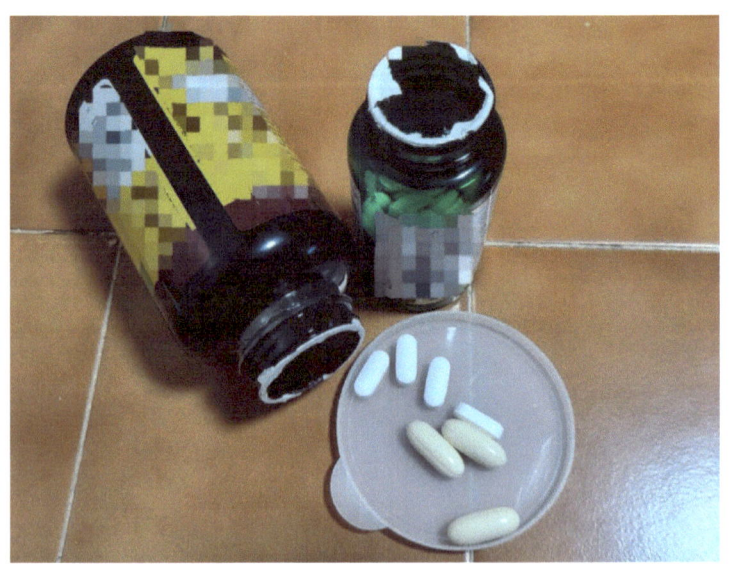

Bakery

A store that sells bread, cake, coffee and tea

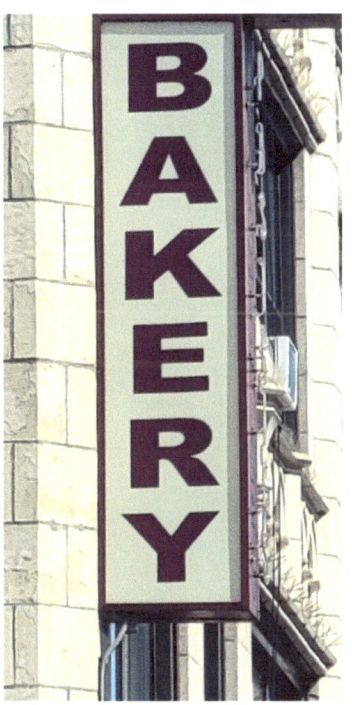

Example of coffee and cake

Bagel Store

A store that sells bagels, coffee and tea

Bagel: a type of bread

Coffee: a hot drink made from ground or roasted coffee beans

Takeout Restaurant

A restaurant that sells food for takeout or to eat in (eat inside)

Chinese Restaurant: a takeout restaurant that sells Chinese food

Container of pork fried rice

Pork fried rice: rice that is fried with pork, eggs, and vegetables

Pizza Shop

A store that sells pizza and pasta

Pizza: baked dough with cheese, meat, or vegetables

Pasta: dough that is made into different shapes and boiled

Cheese, meat, or spices are added to make pasta dishes

Cash Only

Cash is only accepted at a store (no debit or credit cards)

Sorry for the inconvenience: apology for difficulty or trouble

Mobile Order Pickup

To place an order (food or drink) from a phone and pick it up at the store

Picking up an order: coffee

No Outside Food or Drinks Allowed

Cannot bring food from a store into another store that sells food

Example of bringing a drink from a store into a coffee shop

Snack Store

A store that sells snacks, soda, coffee, and cigarettes

Example of snacks

Snacks (junk food): a small amount of food to eat between meals

Discount Store

A store that sells items for a cheaper price

Dishes: plates, cups, and pots are sold at a discount store

Gift Store

A store that sells a variety of things to give as gifts

Gifts are things we give to people

Flowers Store

A store that sells different types of flowers

Flowers: a part of a plant that blossoms

Examples of different types of flowers

Roses

Sunflowers

Wines-Liquors Store

A store that sells different types of alcohol

Wine: an alcoholic drink made from grapes

Shoe Store

A store that sells different types of shoes

Shoes: a cover for feet that is made of leather and a sole (inside bottom of shoes) to protect the feet

Nail Salon

A place to get fingernails and toenails cleaned, shaped, and polished

Nail polish: a varnish to put on fingernails and toenails

Beauty Supply Store

A store that sells makeup, jewelry, hair, and hair products

Makeup   **Hair**

Wigs (fake hair)

Brush and Comb: use to keep hair neat

Jewelry: ornaments to put on the body

Necklaces: wear around the neck

Barber Shop

A place to get a haircut

Inside a barber shop

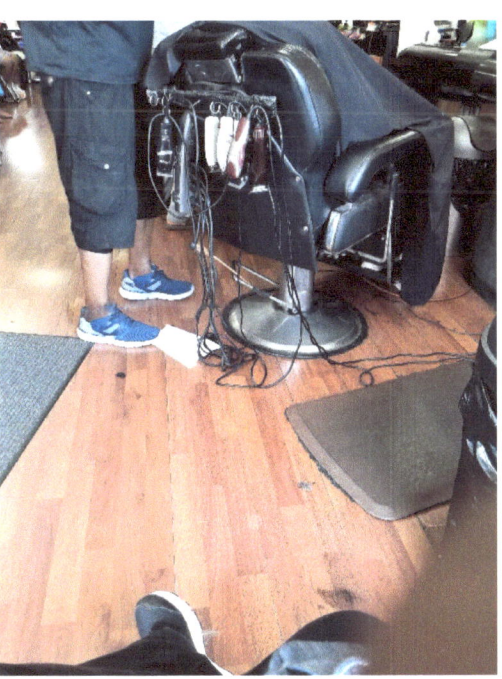

Example of a haircut

Hardware Store

A store to buy things for the home or to fix things

Keys: use to open doors

We can get keys made at a hardware store

Furniture Store

A store that sells tables, chairs, mattresses, things for the home

Types of furniture

Desk: a type of furniture to read, write or do work on

Mattress: a large, rectangular shaped pad for people to sleep on

Wireless-Electronics Store

A store that sells electronics and wireless devices

Examples of wireless devices

Cell phone/Smartphone

Tablet

To make calls, go on social media, or use the internet

Examples of electronics

Cameras: to take pictures

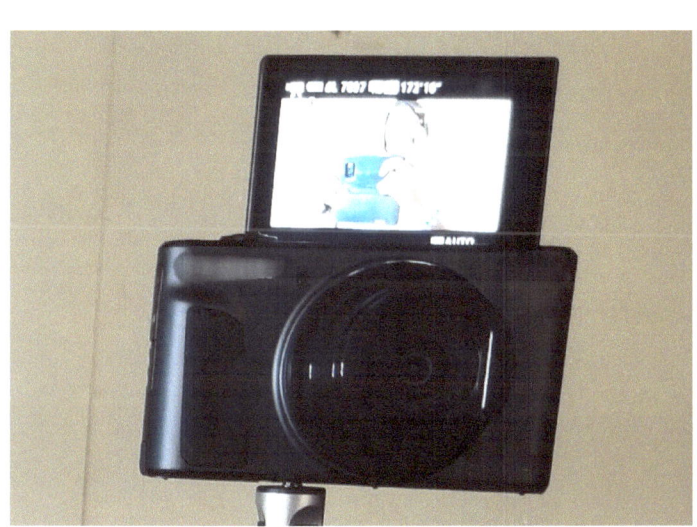 

Television (TV)

Movie Theater

A place to watch movies

Movie Theater Rules

Customers must buy a ticket to enter the theater and keep their ticket stub while at the theater

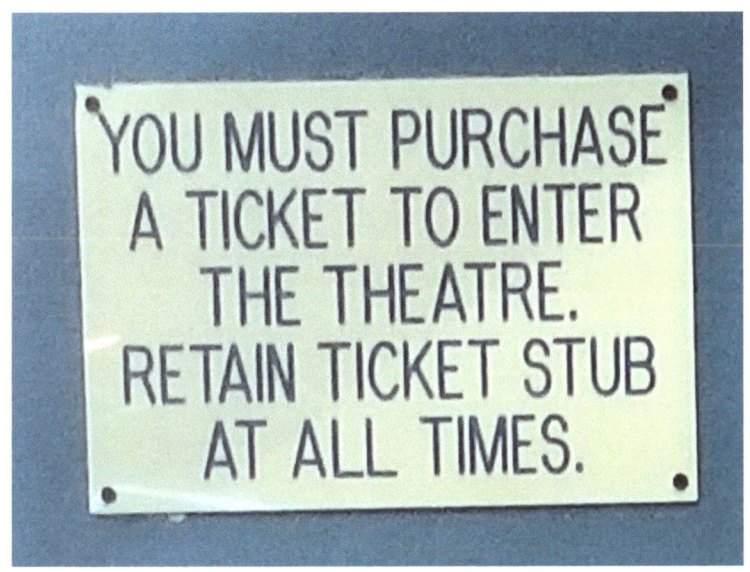

*Theater and Theatre have the same meaning

Movie ticket: shows the name of the movie, date and time, and theater number

No talking on your cell phone is allowed during the movie

Pagers must be turned on silent mode during the movie

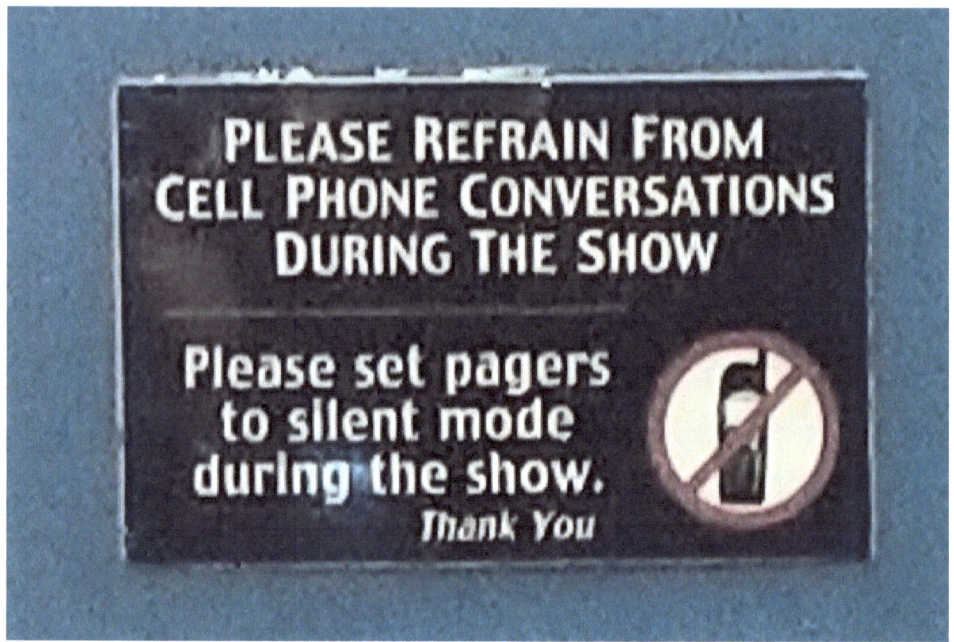

Silent mode: to put your phone on silent (no ringing)

***Pagers, also known as beepers, are no longer common**

No hanging around (loitering), smoking or alcohol are allowed at the movie theater

Printing Store

A store to make copies of documents

Passport Photos Store

A store to take a photo for a passport

It may take 1 hour or less to process a passport photo

Passport: a government identification (ID) that is used for international travel

Passport photo: a picture for a passport

Dry Cleaners and Alterations

A store that cleans and repairs different types of clothing

Example of clothes from a dry cleaners and receipt

A dry cleaner's receipt shows the amount of money paid for the service, the date and time of pickup, and the location of the dry cleaners

Laundromat

A place to wash and dry clothes

Wash machine: to wash clothes

Dryers: to dry clothes

Laundry: clothes to wash

Pharmacy

A store to buy medicine and to fill (to complete) and pick up prescriptions

Prescriptions

Written instructions by a doctor to a patient about treatment or medicine for an illness

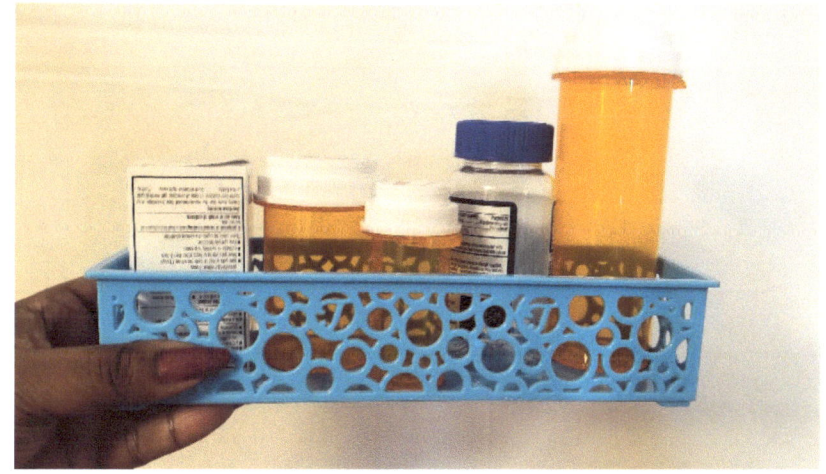

Optical Store

A store to buy eyeglasses and to get an eye exam

Eyeglasses: a pair of lenses inside frames that sit on the nose and ears of the face that helps a person to see

Example of an eye exam

Medical Office

A place to see the doctor

Waiting room

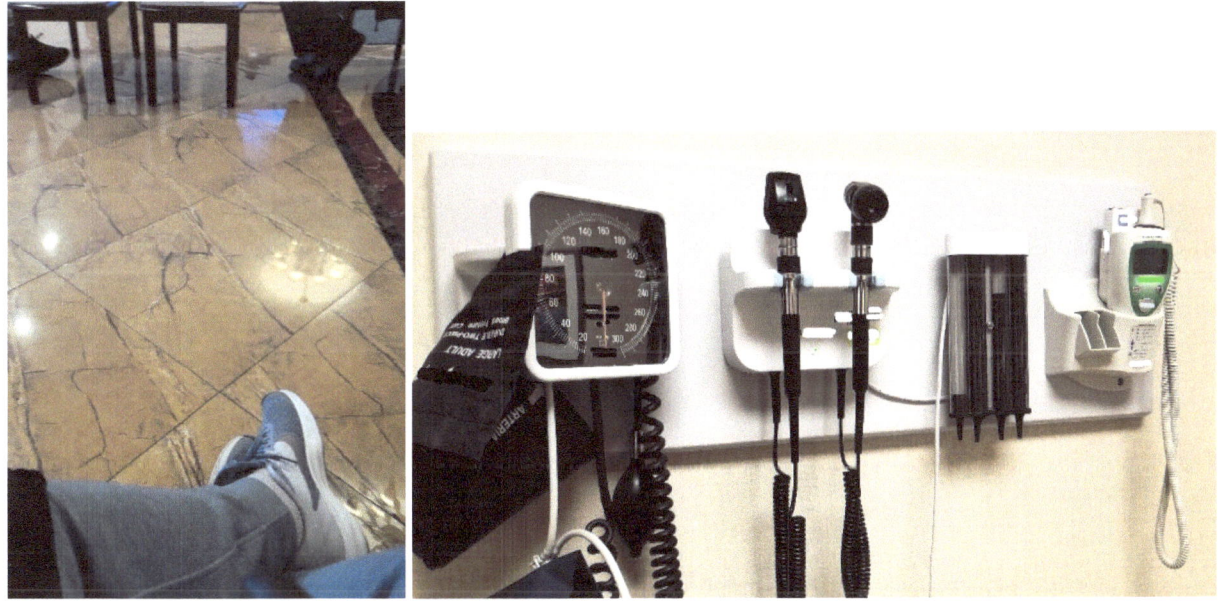

Exam room: a room where the doctor will examine a patient

Emergency Room at a Hospital

A room in a hospital that treats patients with illnesses and health emergencies

A hospital is a place for people who are sick, hurt or need immediate care

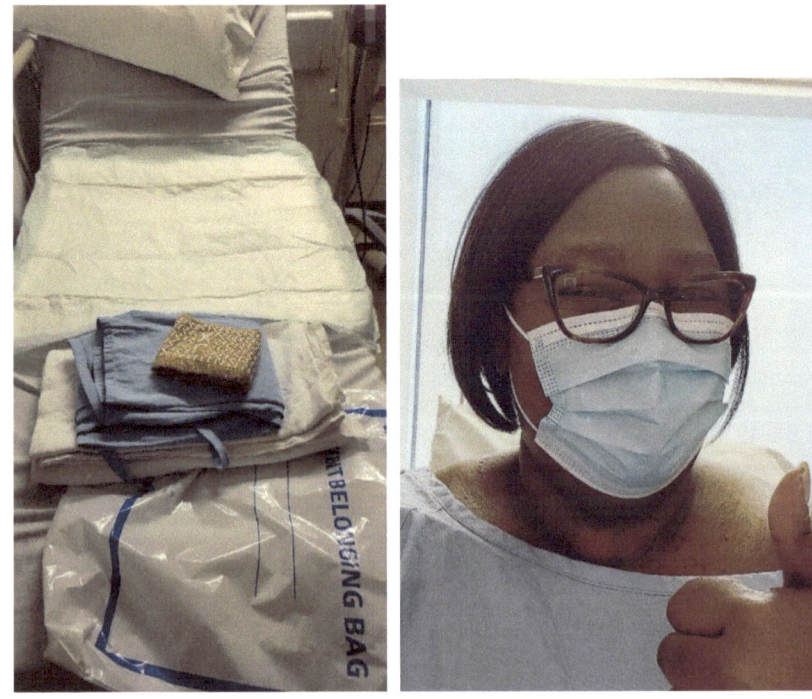

Example of a hospital bed with a bag for patient's clothes, a gown and socks for a patient

Pull for Help

A cord to pull for an emergency or need assistance from a nurse

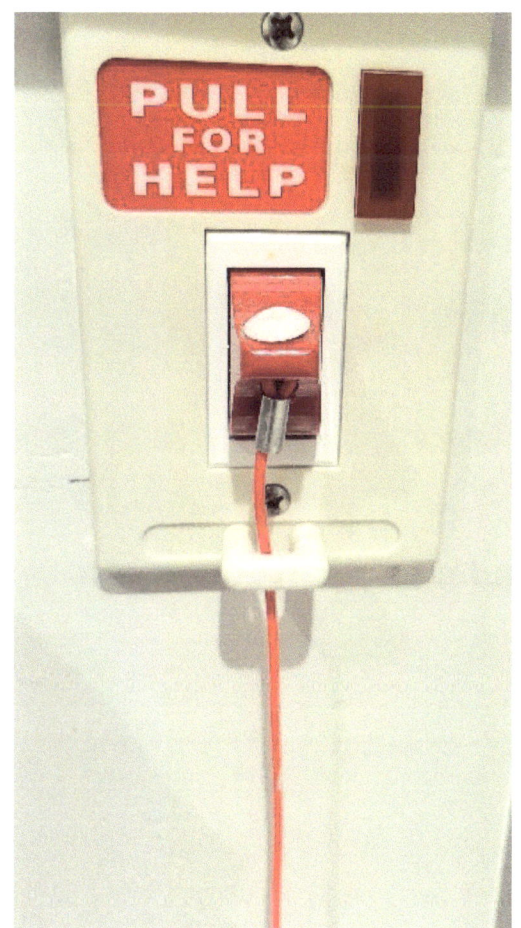

This is inside of a hospital (or doctor's office) bathroom

Dental Office

A place to see the dentist

A dentist is a doctor that examines your teeth

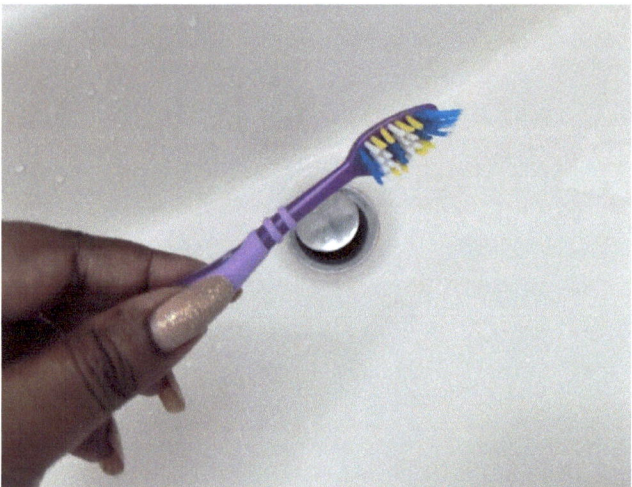

Toothbrush: a brush with a long handle to clean your teeth

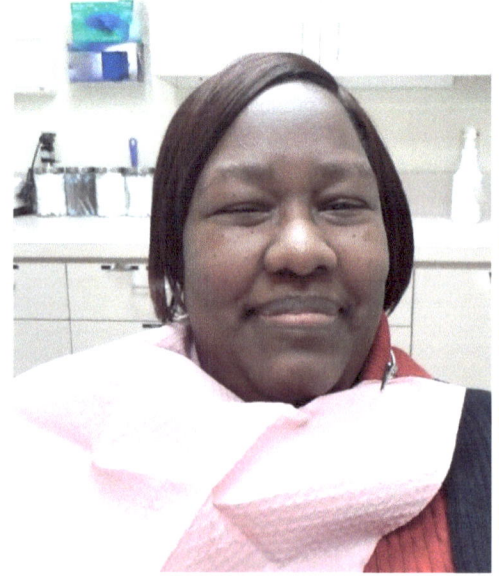

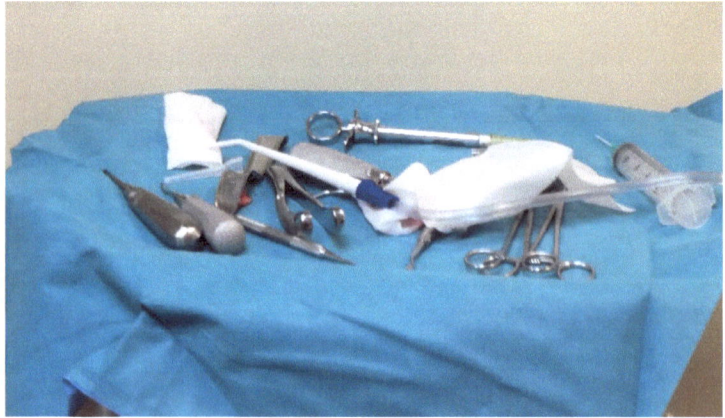

Example of a dental exam and procedure

Newsstand

A stand that sells newspapers and snacks

Newspapers: printed publications that contain news articles (current events) and advertisements

Restaurant Equipment

A place to buy equipment for restaurants and their kitchens

Example of restaurant kitchen equipment

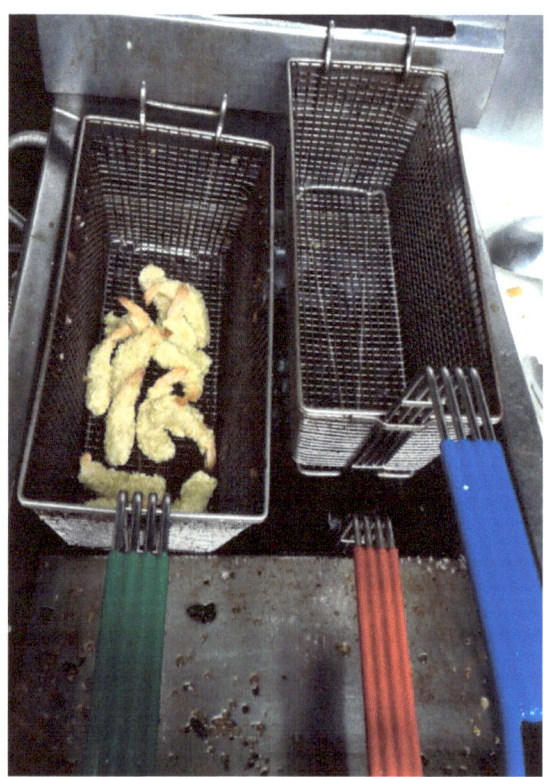

A fryer is a large basket or container to fry food

Flat Fix

A place to buy or get car tires fixed

Tires: Rubber around a wheel used for cars and other vehicles

Car Service

A place to request car service

Car service: a service where drivers pick up passengers to drive them to their destination

Passengers must wear a seatbelt because it is the law in New York

Driving School

A place to learn how to drive

Students take a certain number of lessons to learn how to drive and to pass the road test

A road test is a driving test to test the student's knowledge of road signs, rules of the road, and how to drive and park a car

Store for Rent

A store that is available for rent

Rent: to pay money monthly or yearly to use a space

For Sale

A store or a place that is available for sale (to buy)

Do Not Enter

Cannot use the escalator

Example of an escalator

This Way to Checkout

Direction to the checkout line

Checkout Line Starts Here

Customers stand in line and wait for the cashier to record the items the customer is purchasing

Exit Stairs-Handicap Checkout

Exit to the stairs or checkout line for customers in a wheelchair or with disabilities

ATM 24 Hour

Automatic Teller Machine: a machine to withdraw (take out) money from a bank card

ATM is available 24 hours a day

Example of an Automatic Teller Machine (ATM)

Check Cashing

A place to cash a check (to get money from a check) and pay a fee for the exchange

Suggestions and Comments Box

A box at a business for customers to write their suggestions and opinions about the business and put it in a box

Customer Service Center Closed

A place that is closed for business because of a holiday

Fourth of July-Independence Day

Independence Day is a national holiday in the United States and most businesses are closed

American flag: a flag that represents the United States

COVID 19 Instructions

COVID-19 (Corona Virus)

A type of virus that is contagious and can cause illnesses

Masks

A cloth that covers the nose and mouth for protection from dust or air pollution

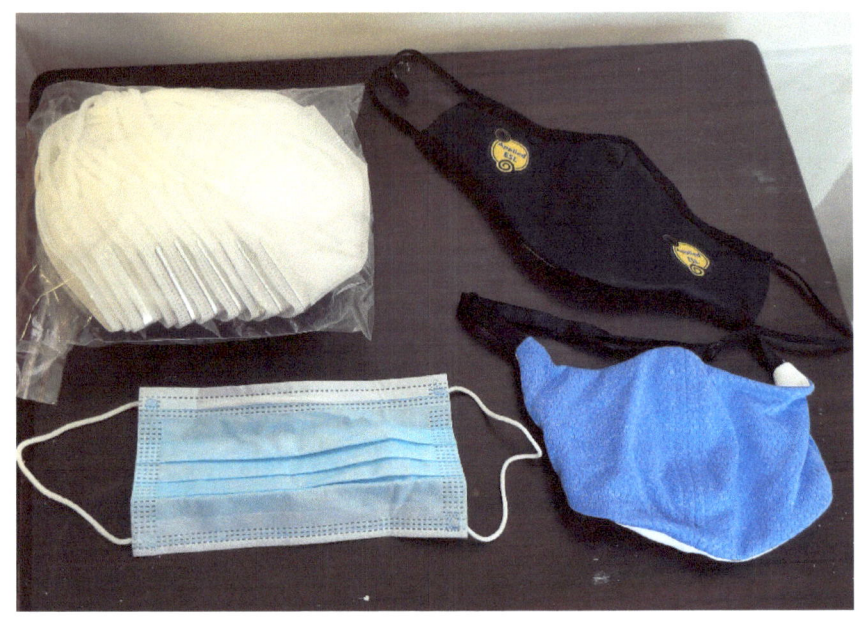

We wear a mask to protect us from getting the corona virus

Social Distancing

To stand 6 feet away from a person

Example of a person social distancing

Examples of social distance signs in stores and businesses

Inside a medical office

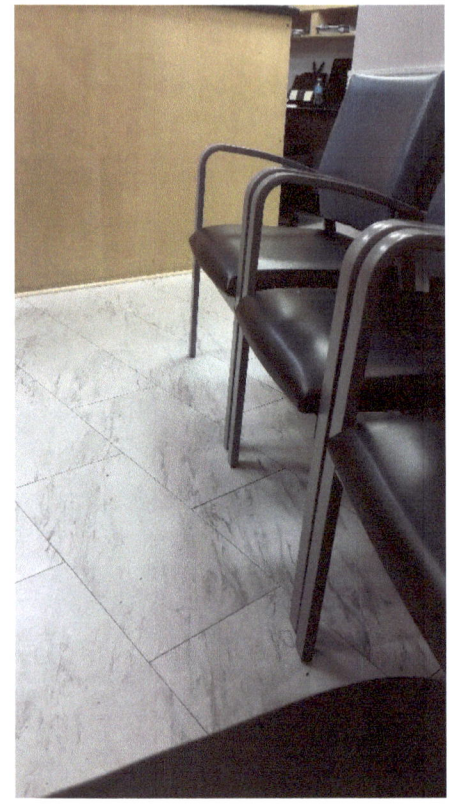

SKIP SEAT FOR SOCIAL DISTANCING

Stay here to be 6 feet apart.

Inside a store

Inside a deli

Inside a taxi

 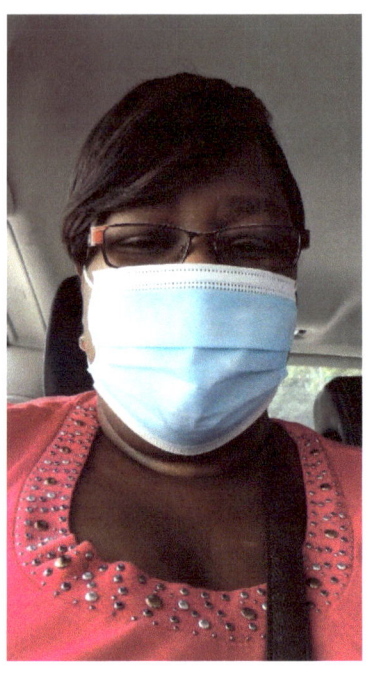

Sign outside of a laundromat

The laundromat is closed for an unknown length of time because of COVID 19

Due to The Safety of Everyone during this COVID-19 Pandemic, We are closing our Laundromat indefinitely until further notice. God bless us All!

Sign outside of a store

The store has temporary store hours due to COVID

The store is closed for a certain amount of days

Signs outside of businesses

People who are not wearing a mask cannot enter

Outdoor Dining

To eat outside

Outdoor dining is preferred during COVID 19 to keep customers and restaurant staff safe

Signs outside of restaurants

People must wear masks before going into a restaurant and be served

Served: to bring food to someone at a restaurant

Some restaurants offer blankets (a large covering to keep you warm) for outdoor dining

COVID 19 Testing

Tests that detect a positive (have COVID) or negative (don't have COVID) result

COVID tests are free and are available at outside clinics, pharmacies or medical offices

COVID 19 Home Tests

COVID 19 tests that people can take at home

COVID-19 TESTS

WE ARE CURRENTLY OUT OF STOCK FOR THE COVID-19 HOME TEST

12/20/2021

Home tests are out of stock (no more available)

Teacher Dara says:

TRY YOUR BEST